Soccer
in
Africa

By
Mike Kennedy
with Mark Stewart

NORWOODHOUSE PRESS

Norwood House Press, P.O. Box 316598, Chicago, Illinois 60631

For information regarding Norwood House Press,
please visit our website at: www.norwoodhousepress.com or call 866-565-2900.

Photo Credits:
    All interior photos provided by Getty Images.
Cover Photos:
    Top Left: Panini.
    Top Right: Laurence Griffiths/FIFA via Getty Images.
    Bottom Left: Clive Rose/Getty Images.
    Bottom Right: Futera FZ LLC.
The soccer memorabilia photographed for this book is part of the authors' collections:
    Page 10) Drogba: Panini.
    Page 12) Eusebio: Panini; Milla: Author's Collection; N'Kono: Panini; Weah: Panini.
    Page 13) Drogba: Futera FZ LLC; Eto'o: Panini; Essien: Topps Trading Cards; Gyan: Panini.

Designer: Ron Jaffe
Project Management: Black Book Partners, LLC
Editorial Production: Jessica McCulloch
Special thanks to Ben and Bill Gould

Library of Congress Cataloging-in-Publication Data
    Kennedy, Mike, 1965-
      Soccer in Africa / by Mike Kennedy, with Mark Stewart.
         p. cm. -- (Smart about sports)
      Includes bibliographical references and index.
      Summary: "An introductory look at the soccer teams and their fans in
    countries in Africa. Includes a brief history, facts, photos, records, and
    glossary"--Provided by publisher.
       ISBN-13: 978-1-59953-441-1 (library ed. : alk. paper)
       ISBN-10: 1-59953-441-X (library ed. : alk. paper)
       1. Soccer--Africa--Juvenile literature. 2. Soccer teams--Africa--Juvenile
    literature. I. Stewart, Mark, 1960- II. Title.
      GV944.A4K46 2011
      796.334096--dc22

                                    2010044551

Manufactured in the United States of America in North Mankato, Minnesota.
170N–012011

Contents

Words in **bold type** are defined on page 24.

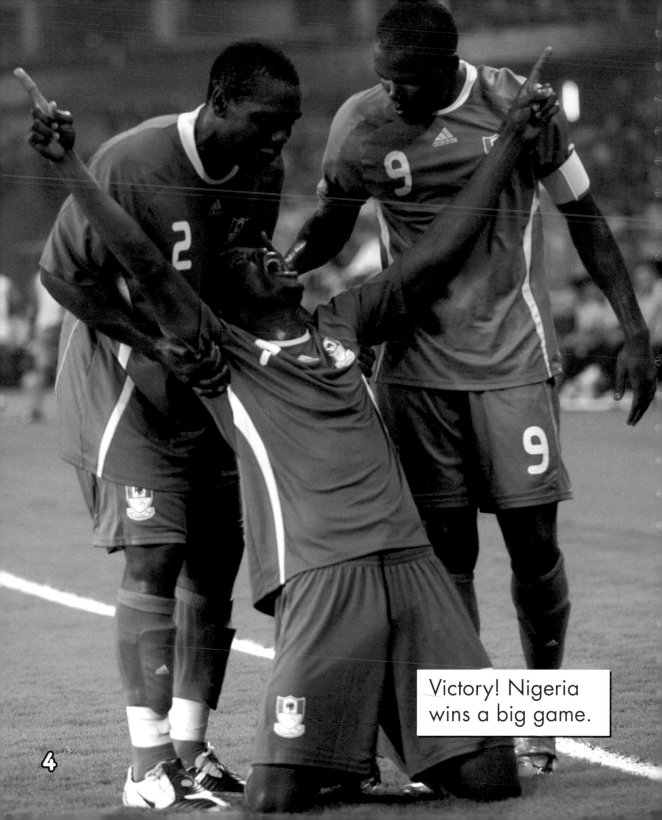

Victory! Nigeria wins a big game.

4

Where in the World?

The people of Africa play
soccer almost anywhere.
They play in wide open
places and narrow streets.
All they need is a ball and
their love of the sport.

Once Upon a Time

Workers and students from Europe brought soccer to Africa in the 1900s. Africans made the game their own. In 2010, the **World Cup** was held in the country of South Africa.

Eusebio was Africa's greatest star.

African fans blow horns called vuvuzelas.

At the Stadium

FNB Stadium in South Africa is the largest stadium in Africa. Fans in the city of Johannesburg call it "The Calabash." They named it after a round plant that can be used as a bottle or jug.

Town & Country

Didier Drogba is famous in countries more than 3,000 miles (4,828 kilometers) apart. In 2010, he was a member of a team in England. He also plays for the Ivory Coast **national team**.

Didier Drogba scores a goal for his English team.

Shoe Box

The soccer collection on these pages belongs to the authors. It shows some of the top African soccer stars.

Eusebio

Forward
- **Mozambique**
Eusebio scored more than 700 goals.

EUSEBIO
(PORTUGAL)

REPUBLIQUE DU CAMEROUN 500F

REPUBLIC OF CAMEROON

COURVOISIER

Roger Milla

Forward • Cameroon
No one had more fun celebrating a goal than Roger Milla.

Thomas N'Kono

Goalkeeper
- **Cameroon**
Thomas N'Kono was Africa's greatest goalkeeper.

CAM

THOMAS N'KONO

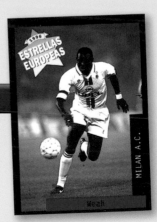

ESTRELLAS EUROPEAS

MILAN A.C.

Weah

George Weah

Striker • Liberia
George Weah was the first African to be named European Player of the Year.

Didier Drogba

Striker • Ivory Coast
Didier Drogba was
a great leader on
and off the field.

Samuel Eto'o

Striker • Cameroon
Samuel Eto'o won
six championships
with his Spanish
team in 2009.

Michael Essien

Midfielder • Ghana
Michael Essien was
strong and tough.
He never seemed
to get tired.

Asamoah Gyan

Striker • Ghana
Asamoah Gyan scored
the winning goal
against Team USA in
the 2010 World Cup.

Can't Touch This

Players are not allowed to touch the ball with their hands. If they do, they are called for a "hand-ball." A hand-ball near your own goal means the other team gets a **penalty kick**.

Samuel Eto'o of Cameroon scores on a penalty kick.

15

Vincent Enyeama
of Nigeria makes
a goal kick.

Just For Kicks

Watching soccer is more fun when you know some of the rules:

- Play stops after a missed shot.

- The team on defense gets the ball after a missed shot.

- Play begins again with a **goal kick**.

- The goalkeeper then kicks the ball to a teammate.

On the Map

Girls and boys play soccer all over Africa, including these countries:

1. Cameroon
2. Egypt
3. Equatorial Guinea
4. Ghana
5. Ivory Coast
6. Liberia
7. Mozambique
8. Nigeria
9. Rwanda
10. South Africa
11. Tanzania

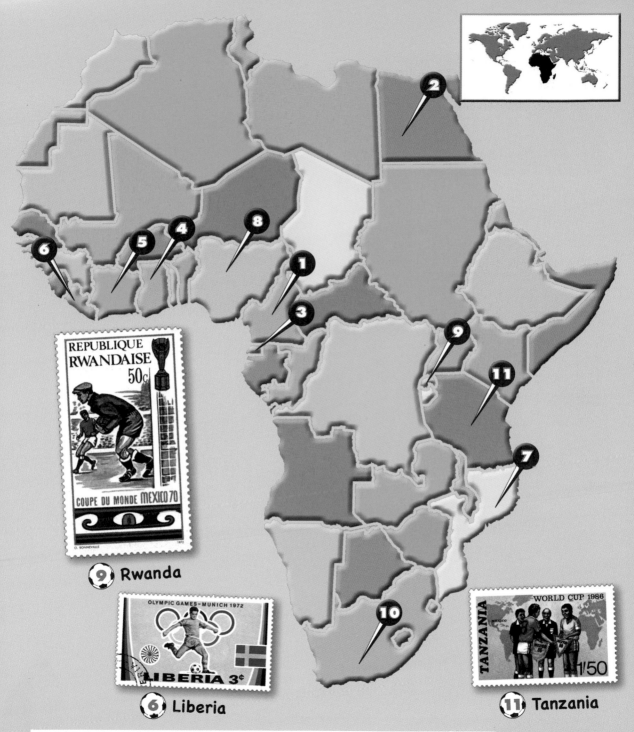

REPUBLIQUE RWANDAISE 50¢

COUPE DU MONDE MEXICO 70

🟡 9 Rwanda

OLYMPIC GAMES—MUNICH 1972

LIBERIA 3¢

⚽ 6 Liberia

TANZANIA — WORLD CUP 1986

1/50

⚽ 11 Tanzania

Many countries have their own soccer stamps!

19

Stop Action

Kaylin Swart of South Africa tries to stop a shot.

Goalkeepers wear padded gloves.

A soccer field is also called a "pitch."

A soccer shirt is also called a "jersey."

21

We Won!

Africa has some of the best teams in the world!

Men's Soccer	African Champion
Egypt	1957, 1959, 1986, 1998, 2006, 2008, & 2010
Ghana	1963, 1965, 1978, & 1982
Nigeria	1980 & 1994
Cameroon	1984, 1988, 2000, & 2002
South Africa	1996

Women's Soccer	African Champion
Nigeria	1991, 1995, 1998, 2000, 2002, 2004, & 2006
Equatorial Guinea	2008

The Nigerian women celebrate in 2006.

Soccer Words

GOAL KICK
A free kick by the goalkeeper.

NATIONAL TEAM
A team made up of players from the same country.

PENALTY KICK
A free shot given to a team after a foul has been called in front of the goal.

WORLD CUP
The tournament that decides the world champion of soccer. The World Cup is played every four years.

Index

Photos are on **bold** numbered pages.

Learn More

Learn more about the World Cup at www.fifa.com

Learn more about men's soccer at www.mlssoccer.com

Learn more about women's soccer at www.womensprosoccer.com